Where Love Is

where Love is

Meditative poems for inspiration and healing

JENNIFER JOY KURTZE

My book is dedicated to my two wonderful children,
David and Kristen, and my gorgeous grandchildren.

My book of poems was not planned.

It seems as if the words were just there, waiting to be written. I know that they came from where love is.

Where Love Is began to emerge in April 2023.

Foreword

I grew up in Garden Street, in the Victorian coastal town of Portland, Australia. My father was a wholesale fruiterer, my mother loved tending her garden, particularly the magnificent rose garden which surrounded our weatherboard home.

Alongside our home was a timber fruit packing shed. As a little girl, I thought the shed was huge and exciting. There were platforms for trucks to load cases of apples and many nooks and crannies to hide in. A big grading machine sorted apples from the family orchard at North Portland. Trucks would come and go as apples were loaded and delivered to shops in Victoria. Sometimes I accompanied my father in his big black truck, as he delivered apples to nearby towns.

It was 1947. I was five years old.

In 2023, I live near Geelong, Victoria, and my home is surrounded by beautiful white rose bushes. The rich earth, the sparkling ocean, the glorious wineries on the surrounding Bellarine Peninsula and the memories of my childhood garden have inspired me to write and share these meditative poems. They come from my heart to yours.

My study, practice, and teaching of meditation over several decades, confirms that love is who we are. I trust this book will be a comforting companion to you. We all have a bubbling brook of creativity within us, when we set it free it will flow. You, like me, may find it liberating. Create your own inspirational words, art or reflections on the Affirmation page. Do this with love.

Jennifer

Carry this book wherever you go,
Your creativity will begin to flow.

Ponder these pure messages
When you feel the need for quiet.
It will be in that still moment
That you recognise your Light.

There's creativity within us all
Just yearning to get out.
Still your mind, tune to heart
Your creativity will shout!

Contents

Transformation

Renewal

What Is Meditation?

Meditation is a natural process which simplifies our life, deepens our happiness and helps us to develop our potential. We can't change the world in which we live but we can change our reaction to it.

By practicing meditation, we create for ourselves a more stress-free life.

A meditative state is reached by allowing our mind to rest for a while, by gently letting go of thoughts, ideas and activity of the mind.

The process of meditation may be achieved by practicing simple and natural breathing techniques. With practice and patience, the outcomes can be very rewarding.

We all meditate in our own way, perhaps when we are walking in a beautiful environment, listening to gentle music or reading inspirational verse.

The poems in this book came to me through meditation. I invite you to reflect upon the prose. As you ponder the words, you may find yourself gently meditating in your own way.

Love

Affirmation:

Real love starts with me.

What Is Love

What is love was asked of me,
Many years ago.
The answer then, was hard to know
I waited for the years to flow.

Love is an energy that glows,
It's you, it's me, expands and grows.
Love feels different year by year,
When we love we have no fear.

Love is deep inside us all
Aways at our beck and call.
Call it God or call it Grace
Love resides in every place.

Divine love makes us feel secure,
It's whole, expansive, good and pure.
Forgiving's easy, judgement fades,
Darkness ends and light pervades.

What is love was asked of me
From someone from my past.
Love is complex, gentle, vast, intriguing,
To my life, love adds all meaning.

What is love to you this day?
Depends on energies at play.
Love is all, it is near and far,
Love is simply, who we are.

Affirmation:

Love flows through me, nourishing my soul.

Soul

My soul is deep inside me,
My pilot and my friend.
It's the place I go for solace,
It's the place that knows no end.

My soul is my true guidance,
My messenger from God.
When I visit my quiet-place,
My heart and mind are agog.

If I'm feeling lonely,
I connect to my wise friend,
This reminds me that I'm home
All my thoughts transcend.

Affirmation:

I breathe in calmness I breathe away stress.

Breath

My breath flows in and through me,
My life-force and my base.
As I meditate upon each breath,
I'm enriched with love and grace.

I take each breath with gratitude,
I feel the fresh, pure air.
I know my breath sustains me.
I Am ... at home ... Aware!

Joy and peace flow through me,
As I take each inward breath.
Out-going breath, I just let go
The tension and distress.

I remind myself life's precious,
As I simply sit and breathe.
I gently rest, enjoy my breath
Release feelings of dis-ease.

No need to make life complex,
Embrace this unique Me.
Enjoy the simple things in life.
Relax. Just be ... Be free.

Affirmation:

I change and remove my limitations.

Heart

Oh, heart you are my treasure,
I access you for peace.
When inside my loving heart
All limitations cease.

Oh, heart you are my solace,
My teacher and my friend.
When within my loving heart
My gratitude knows no end.

Affirmation:

I choose peace.

Peace

Peace at times eludes me,
What to do I ask,
Try to still my active mind,
Tune to my loving heart.

My heart is filled with peace and love,
My mind is filled with thoughts,
Transformation is the key,
My heart's there for support.

Meditate, my heart says
Come inside, be still,
Rest in quiet seclusion
There you'll get your fill.

Thanks for the reminder, heart,
That you are always there,
There to fill my mind with peace,
I shall aim to be aware.

Affirmation:

Breathe, trust, live.

My Heart Garden

When my mind is filled with chatter
It's hard to go to sleep.
I see a garden in my heart
A place that's hidden, deep.

I venture there to rest a while,
Smell the fragrance of sweet flowers.
Feel the breath of gentle breeze,
Part of the floating clouds.

Joy and peace abundantly
Abide in that quiet place.
When I enter my heart garden,
I am feeling love and grace.

Affirmation:

I release doubt and welcome faith.

Guide

Hope is where the heart is,
I can be sad or free.
When I tune into my loving heart
It's only good I see.

Why be sad and lonely?
When there's so much love inside,
I simply open my heart door
It's there, I'm with my guide.

My heart holds all the answers,
They're accessible to me.
Don't listen to my doubting mind
It's my heart that holds the key.

Affirmation:

I am confident, happy and healthy.

Confidence

Please don't leave it 'till too late,
Let your light shine bright.
Recognise your unique worth
Now the time is right.

Follow your dreams, you are worthwhile,
Avoid the doubting mind.
Tune into your loving heart,
A well of love to find.

Love will get you everything.
Everything you need,
Have faith in your ability,
With trust you will succeed.

Affirmation:

I trust my Inner-Guidance.

A Garden in My Heart

I have a place I go to
When my mind is running wild.
This place is called my heart-garden
It's safe and quiet inside.

My heart-garden holds the essence
Of who I really am.
A soul, divine and sacred,
It's where my life began.

When peace of mind eludes me,
I go to my quiet place.
Peace restored,
Life adored,
I'm feeling love and grace.

Affirmation:

All is well in my world now.

Unable to Sleep

I have a place to go to when I can't fall asleep,
That place is deep inside of me, to that place I creep,
Love and peace embrace me, as I enter my heart space.
I'm reminded that I'm guided.
Now filled with love and grace.

Affirmation:

I value myself.

Nurture

In everyday society
Self-love is not encouraged,
It's often seen as selfish
This notion I discourage.

My body is my temple
It's the place that holds my soul,
Love and self-care are a must
For me to reach my goal.

Maintenance is everything
Food, exercise and rest,
Compassion, fun, and quiet time.
It's worth putting to the test.

Self-love is important
It's how my life should be.
To love all others adequately,
My first love must be me.

Affirmation:

I embrace every part of my body.

Connect Within

Its love that makes me happy.
The love that's within me.
When I connect to my within
My Guidance sets me free.

If I feel downhearted,
I stop, take stock, be still.
I connect to my most sacred place,
It's there I get my fill.

Get my fill of gratitude,
Of comfort and of joy,
The love that lives within my heart
Will never be destroyed.

My soul journey has a mission,
Which was planned before my birth.
My mind may try to sabotage,
Make me forget my worth.

Forget my worth! ... No never!
That would not be smart.
I'll bring transformation to my mind,
Make it wise, just like my heart.

Affirmation:

I only compare myself to myself.

Gratitude

My heart is filled with gratitude,
My life is filled with love,
I see beauty all around me,
Below, across, above.

I'm grateful for the goodness
Which surrounds me every day.
Gratitude is everywhere,
It makes me want to pray.

To say thank you to the cosmos
For giving me this chance.
To contribute to enlightenment,
To help the world advance.

I'm here for a good reason,
To learn, to grow, to serve.
I'll try to do my very best.
This world I must preserve.

Affirmation:

Anything is possible.

Oneness

When I choose to meditate
I go into my heart,
I then begin to realize
Of this world I am a part.

I feel the Light that flows within,
Light also flows without.
Light flows around me everywhere
That's what this world's about.

If I feel downhearted
Or somehow overwhelmed.
Peaks and troughs are part of life
Through faith I will transcend.

Have faith and trust in who I am
Embrace this unique Me.
Recognise the world is love,
Loving sets me free.

Affirmation:

I am divinely guided by the Universe.

The Universe Within

I have a place within me
It is wide, and deep and vast.
When I connect to my within
Of this world I am a part.

Affirmation:

*Every day is a gift. I don't have
to understand everything.*

Light

I see a Light above me
It flickers and it glows,
It changes shape
It comes and goes,
Purple, silver, green and gold.
I don't have to understand it
Just embrace … And feel.
It feels so good and wholesome,
I'm feeling grateful to be me.

Affirmation:

I am protected.

Aura

I see a sparkling aura
I feel a sense of awe
It brings feelings of protection
Love rises to the fore.

Affirmation:

The Universe is always working for my better good.

What Can I Do?

What can I do for a suffering world
Remember that I'm a small part,
If I can send love and Light,
I'm doing my best.
I trust in the Universal Heart.

Affirmation:

I was created with a divine intention.

Who Am I?

I tune into the magnificence
Of who I really am.
A soul divine and sacred,
Part of a divine plan.

I marvel at the beauty
Of the body I live in,
Not so much the outward,
But the beauty from within.

It's easy to condemn myself,
I will stop doing this.
It's an insult to creation,
Which is filled with perfect bliss.

This work of art's extraordinary,
As is all upon this earth.
Gratitude for everything,
Particularly my birth.

Affirmation:

If it has to be its up to me.

The Musk Deer

The world is bad, I have heard said.
What could make it good?
It is only love that makes the change
Why is this not understood?

We search for love in every place,
Forgetting it's within.
There's Light and love in all of us.
When we realize this, we'll win.

There's a story of a musk deer
Who smelt a fragrant smell,
He ran, and ran, in search of it,
Until he realized it was within.

The fragrance of love
Is within us all,
Simply, set it free
Then the world's in perfect peace.
It's really up to me.

Affirmation:

The Universal plan is limitless. I do my best.

I Do My Best

I often wonder what to do
To make our world a better place,
When I watch the news, I see stories
Of people who're displaced.

As I sit in my warm lounge room
With my coffee and fresh food,
How can I help others?
Some comfort to include.

I recognise there's a plan for all,
But how can I invest
Some good into this world of ours,
To make conditions best.

I've learnt what makes the world restored
Is simply care and love,
Love becomes so clouded
When on the back burner it's shoved.

Perhaps, it just comes back to me,
To offer help wherever I can
Send loving thoughts across the world,
All judgment I will ban.

Trust the Universal Heart
Because it does know best.
Embrace vastness and the oneness.
It won't help others if I'm stressed.

My Heart Garden Meditation

Please find a comfortable place to sit.
Allow your body to relax and feel at ease.
Recognise and embrace the goodness within YOU.
Visualise your body becoming filled with love and peace.

Take a deep breath ....
Feel that you are drawing serene energy into your body.
Notice the healing energy gently flowing
throughout your entire being.
Relax your body.
On the outgoing breath, let go of tension ....
Try to let go of anything which does not serve you well.

Establish a flow of the breath which feels comfortable for you.
Enjoy the gentle rhythmic flow of your breath.

Emagine you are sitting quietly in a beautiful garden.
Feel at peace, as you bathe in the serenity of your garden.
You may hear birds singing, or feel a gentle breeze.
Feel at peace as you become relaxed.

Quietly continue to follow your breath,
naturally, in your own way.
If your mind becomes filled with thoughts and ideas.
Gently bring your attention back to your breath.

Feel a sense of oneness with nature as you
rest in the serenity of your garden.
Know that you are loved and supported.
Be gentle on yourself.
Think of this garden as your Heart Garden.
Your Heart Garden is *WHERE LOVE IS.*
You can open the door, go inside, find peace, whenever you wish.

Transformation

Affirmation:

I am enough.

Depression

When skies are grey and stormy
The world seems grim and dark.
My mind says, I'm a part of this
My heart says, time to start.

Start to see the Light within
The Light transforms the gloom.
The world is never meant to be
Like a darkened room.

It's up to me to make the change,
My optimism takes flight.
My heart is filled with love and good
My body is feeling right.

I remind myself I have the strength
To overcome my fears.
Perceptions change with every breath,
My guidance always hears.

The Universal Heart is large,
It's filled with love and peace.
Its people who create the change,
And make the grey clouds cease.

Affirmation:

I feel joy, I am joy, I become joy.

Joy

As I gaze across the ocean,
I feel a sense of joy,
The world is quiet,
The sun is bright.
In touch with Inner-Pilot.

I see the vast horizon,
Expand in front of me.
I feel a sense of oneness,
I am completely free.

The joy of having quiet time
In this world of noise and rush,
Rejuvenates my body.
I'm glad to be in touch.

Affirmation:

The Universe laughs with me.

Laughter

Laughter is a medicine
That I should take each day,
The inward life is magical,
Combined with fun and play.

Balance is the greatest key,
To creating life at best,
Walking, dancing, social dates,
With a little bit of rest.

Laughter makes endorphins
Come rising to the fore,
It strengthens my immunity
And leaves me wanting more.

Laughter is my birthright,
It's contagious, it's a must.
Best of all its priceless,
My budget it won't bust.

Affirmation:

I radiate purity and grace.

Purity

My being is filled with purity,
My heart is filled with Light.
My soul, within is the deity
Uniting brings delight.

Affirmation:

I give myself permission to grow and learn.

Mind

My mind says I'm not good enough,
My heart says come inside,
Come to where its Light-filled,
Not to a place of pride.

Pride and ego limit me,
This doesn't give me peace,
When I'm living in my heart
All limitations cease.

My heart brings transformation,
My mind says, I know best.
When I can unite the two,
I have no more unrest.

Affirmation:

I am in charge.

Fear

Fear I will let go of.
It contaminates my peace,
When I choose to go within
My fearful thoughts will cease.

Fear can freely be transformed,
Replaced with love and faith,
I simply need to access
My inner-sacred-place.

If I'm feeling fearful,
I connect to my wise friend,
My mind will then be made at ease,
All fearful thoughts transcend.

When fear overtakes me,
The choice is mine to make.
Do I choose fear to bring me down,
Or replace with trust and faith.

Affirmation:

I exhale worry and inhale trust.

Hope

Sometimes the world around seems bleak,
With droughts, floods, lack, and war.
I wonder what I can do to change,
To make our world restored.

The only thing that I can change
In this world is me.
Make the changes where I can
Offer help where I foresee.

I see wonder all around me,
Sunshine, grass and trees,
Remind myself of earth's support
Bring our land some ease.

Keep my mind more positive
Tune deep into my heart.
Offer love and healing where I can
Is somewhere I can start.

I want my world to be at peace
That's what I strive to see.
I do believe for this to be
It has to start with me.

Affirmation:

I love the person I'm becoming.

Mood

Sometimes I feel excited,
Excited to be me.
Other times my mood is low
Quiet, I have to be.

I recognise I'm human,
I ride the peaks and troughs.
Life is a simply but a game,
Why get tied in knots?

I have a peaceful heart-space
To go when I need peace,
I make time to sit quietly and relax
Content to just be me.

Affirmation:

A bad moment can be changed now.

Body and Spirit

I am more than just a body,
I'm a Light-filled spirit being.
I keep my thoughts more positive,
This helps my self-esteem.

My mind reflects the mood I'm in,
I keep vibrations high,
I keep this body well maintained,
Which makes my spirit fly.

Affirmation:

*My most challenging moments
are a catalyst for change.*

Attitude

My attitude is everything,
I can feel good or feel bad.
I can be critical of others,
Or kind and feeling glad.

My thoughts are all contagious,
I must be mindful of my views,
Keep my thoughts more positive,
Not condemn and disapprove.

When I value my uniqueness,
And am grateful for my life,
I make my world a better place.
That's my best advice.

Affirmation:

I release judgment of others now.

Race

We're a universal family,
One race, one mob, one creed.
Some countries have abundance,
Others are in need.

We're all interconnected,
Under one eternal sun,
When we judge others for their colour,
Justice is not done.

We are all born with kind hearts,
What happens to make change?
What makes people angry?
... Act with such outrage.

Our lives, they are a blessing
From wherever we may come,
Behaving without kindness
Is acting rather dumb.

Affirmation:

I am proud of myself for everything I have overcome.

Restoration Garden

I have a place to go to when I'm feeling flawed,
This place is called my Heart-Garden
when I visit, I'm restored.

Affirmation:

I am feeling better.

Heart Garden Fountain

Inside my heart's a peaceful place,
Bright flowers, sun, fresh air.
It even has a fountain,
Which washes away my cares.

I stand beneath my fountain,
I feel cleansed and free, I breathe.
It's great to have a peaceful place,
Deep inside of me.

The glistening water's magical,
I bathe my hair and skin
My muscles relax, my cells renew.
I feel harmony within.

Affirmation:

I trust the world.

Meditation

What is meditation was asked of me today,
Not for me to answer, it happens in our own way.
Silence is our birthright, that's what meditation is,
It's simply when Source answers
when we choose to go within.

Answers come through silence. It's good to just be still,
To eliminate the chatter. Our soul, it does fulfill.
It really isn't complex, I do it every day.
It can be when I'm walking or even when I pray.

My mind may say it's difficult, I'll listen to my heart.
I'll let my thoughts just fade away, all tension will depart.
Meditation's natural, the teacher is within,
Confidence and strength maintained.
A good place to begin.

Affirmation:

Only good things await me.

Separate

When I'm feeling separate
I go into my heart.
It's there I feel the world within,
Of the universe I'm part.

The cosmos, it supports me
I will support it too.
Feeling separate, not for me,
In my heart, I am renewed.

Affirmation:

I confidently welcome new experiences.

Challenges

Challenges come to each of us at some time or another.
No one likes to feel dis-ease. The body will recover.
Handicaps come to us, to help in growth and change.
Peaks and troughs are part of life. Tools to rearrange.

Vulnerability challenges us. It makes us pause and think
Can I do things in a better way to keep my health in sync?
The main thing to remember, there is a sacred plan for all,
The divine within is always there, at my beck-and-call.

When I begin to slow my pace and focus on my health,
I realise that my peace of mind and
breath are my real wealth.
Happiness comes from within me,
not from external things,
When I choose to remember this, restored health begins.

Affirmation:

I am motivated, confident and manage my time well.

Eighty

OMG I'm eighty. No, now, I'm eighty-one!
Mind tells me, I'm over the hill.
Heart says, you're on a run.
Don't listen to your mind dear one,
Listen to your heart.
You can achieve most anything.
Your time is not yet done.

You have a heart of gold, Dear.
We all have a loving heart,
All we simply have to do
Is to make a positive start.
Don't listen to the knockers.
Listen to your friends.

Most importantly, know your worth,
It's your time to excel.
You have a friend within, Dear.
That friend will nourish you.
That loving friend within your heart.
Will see you through and though.

Affirmation:

I trust the messages from my soul.

Eighty-One

Please don't lose your confidence
My heart says to me today
My mind says I'm not good enough.
... Throw that thought away.

I want to write a book.
What! You're eighty-one says mind!
Heart says you can do it,
Mind only wants to bind.

This book, you are now reading
Please don't listen to your mind.
Listen to your loving heart,
Let your creativity shine.

Affirmation:

I feel confident in my body.

Body

My body is my temple
It's here to house my Soul.
I'll honour its uniqueness
Until I reach my goal.

Goals are written within my Soul,
Accessible when quiet.
The messages will all emerge
When the time is right.

My body is a miracle,
To nurture is a must.
The simple things it likes the most,
Its messages I'll trust.

My body will support me,
I shall nurture it in return.
Balance, in my daily life
Is what I'm here to learn.

Affirmation:

I am grateful for the people in my life.

Blessings

I have many blessings,
But sometimes I forget.
I am drawn to superficial things
Forget what suits me best.

Blessings are the people
Who I have within my life,
People I can share with
To keep me out of strife.

My mind sometimes goes awry,
To get it back on track
I call my soul-group friends, and chat.
Then my peace comes back.

Affirmation:

Today is a gift and I shall live it with gratitude.

Grateful

Gratitude is everything
What if I feel poor?
Find something that I'm grateful for
Peace comes knocking at my door.

Affirmation:

Creativity is abundant in my world.

Creativity

I'm a creative artist
In some way or another,
My mind, it tries to block it
My heart says, must discover.

Uncover your creative flare
Let your Light shine bright.
Your art brings joy to others,
Time now to excite.

To excite your senses.
Paint, draw, write … or run!
Whatever you are drawn to do
Let yourself have fun.

Become what you are meant to be
Unique, brave and great.
Tune in to your guidance.
It's your time to create.

Affirmation:

Harmony is developing.

War and Peace

I was asked to write a verse on war.
Fear came to my mind.
Gratitude, brave soldiers,
And to those who were left behind.

I pondered further upon world war,
The duality is peace.
Peace is what I strive to be,
I'd like all war to cease.

Perhaps if we all felt at peace,
There would be no need for war.
I know brave soldiers fought for me,
To keep my life restored.

If peace was in the deciders' heart,
Then war would be no more.
The thought of war flows forth from fear,
... Protect this land. It's mine!

Peace begins when we lose our fears,
The duality is faith.
Ignite the power that lies within,
Let expectation cease.

Affirmation:

I trust my Inner Guidance.

Transforming Chaos

What's happening to the world of ours?
It's busy, rush, rush, rush.
There are people hurrying everywhere
I feel completely out of touch.

I need a little bit of peace.
Where do I find that?
Everyone around seems
Completely out of whack!
I look to find a place to sit.
To quieten down my mind.

I turn my back toward the crowds,
Gaze frontwards and behind,
I glance toward the sky and see
There's only vastness here.

Vastness, trees and singing birds,
Some sunshine and some clouds.
It feels so very different,
When away from all the crowds.

If I need some peace and quiet,
It's simply up to me,
I find a place to sit and be
… Be completely free.

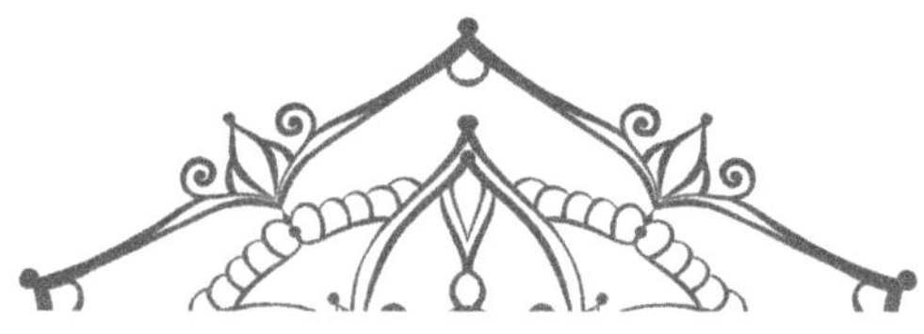

Affirmation:

*I acknowledge destructive patterns,
and actively seek solutions.*

Power

When I give away my power
It leaves me vulnerable to dis-ease.
I'm left with drained energy.
When I'm too eager to please.

It's an unsupportive pattern
Which stems from flawed belief.
I must learn to place high value
Upon myself. I am unique.

This pattern can be limiting
But I can change all that.
By acknowledging my goodness,
I am quickly back on track.

It may be good to speak to
A wise supportive friend,
A person who is always there
Who cares, and has my back.

Friendships come and friendships go,
This is clear to see.
There is no other friendship,
Like the friend inside of me.

Affirmation:

*I accept myself and other people's
right to be themselves.*

Consciousness

I reflect upon the countries I have visited through life,
Each one has a different feel, I often wonder why.
Would it be the people with vibrations high or low?
Or perhaps it is the sacred earth. I guess I'll never know.

In the West we seem to rush, in the East, a slower pace.
It feels so different wherever I go, whatever creed or race.
I experience new cultures when I visit diverse lands,
I reflect upon the different feel, as I stand upon new sand.

It seems that human consciousness
feels different everywhere.
Some people have grand houses, others, sparse and bare.
I think about a turtle with his house upon his back,
He doesn't need possessions and finds
his food along the track.

Energy flows throughout the world, it can be dark or light.
Our thoughts, they are contagious,
let's aim to keep them bright.
The world is made of Yin and Yang, as are people too.
When we keep our thoughts more positive,
higher consciousness is renewed.

Renewal Meditation

The past is dust.
I start my day now.
I embrace the Goodness within me,
I am pure love.
My heart is filled with gratitude,
My life is filled with love.
I see beauty all around me,
Below, across, above.
I am at peace.

Renewal

Affirmation:

What colour comes to your mind?
Write a story about it.

Yellow

A little bit of yellow
Fills my cup today.
The sun is bright
The air feels light
Blue, shimmers on the bay.

My heart feels young and joyful
As I walk the golden sand,
I can't help feeling grateful
To live in this great land.

The joys of life surround me,
My senses feel them all.
The touch, the smells,
The tastes, the sounds.
Delights, all at my call.

Life's a precious privilege,
My mind says today.
My heart feels light,
The world feels right,
It's time to laugh and play.

Affirmation:

Every day is a gift.

Sunrise

I visualise a sunrise
And feel a fresh new dawn,
Time now to let go of past
And start a brand-new morn.

The magic glow surrounds me,
It's yellow, orange hue.
The colour flows into my being
My life, I now review.

I reflect upon the splendour
That surrounds me on this day,
I feel the Light inside me
So many vibrant rays.

I'm reminded of my value.
Being placed here on the earth
To learn, to grow, to reap and sow.
All planned before my birth.

Affirmation:

My body, mind and spirit are free when in nature.

Connect to Nature

What does nature teach me?
It teaches many things.
It teaches me to slow down
Feel the goodness that it brings.

Appreciate the energy that I have within.
Share it with the world around,
Make my spirit sing.
Nature is my solace,
My refuge and my friend.

When I connect to nature,
All my fears transcend.
When in nature, I feel wholeness
I feel nurtured and renewed.

Nature is my magic place,
Nature lifts my mood.
I'm a part of nature,
It's a part of me.
Feel the oneness nature brings.
Embrace nature and feel free.

Affirmation:

I am one with nature.

Seasons

Seasons are enthralling.
I watch them come and go,
Nature offers perfect gifts,
Keeps us naturally in flow.

Summer brings bright sunshine,
Autumn coloured leaves,
Winter brings fresh raindrops,
Spring comes, when Winter leaves.

Synchronicity in abundance,
Seasons are in flow,
Mother Earth brings nourishment,
Offering sustenance to grow.

Affirmation:

I respect all living things.

Trees

When I stand beneath a spreading tree
I hear a gentle call,
It's just a tender whisper,
A sound I wistfully recall.

I feel the subtle energy
The tree so freely shares,
Somehow, I feel more energized
And so much more aware.

Aware of the connection
Between trees and human-beings.
My body, it feels grounded,
And, yes, much more at ease.

Thank you, tree, for being there
To give me breath and shade.
I feel safe, secure, beneath your boughs
In this haven you have made.

I shall be more aware of trees
As I walk my path through life.
Trees bring feelings of infinity
Of life-force and of Light.

Affirmation:

I am one with nature and nature is one with me.

Magpie

I hear a magpie warbling
As she sits upon my fence.
She seems to have a message
Her singing seems intense.

As I see her stand before me
I think of Yin and Yang.
The balance of her black and white
Brings a nostalgic pang.

A nostalgic pang of comfort
As I think of bygone days,
I think about the loved ones
Who have gone and passed away.

The magpie wants to linger
There are things she wants to share,
I give her food and water
She then flies away up there.

Affirmation:

Love is the meaning of life.

Love Is Everywhere

Please don't feel sad
When it's time for me to go.
Just enjoy the memories
Of how much I loved you so.

My life with you - a blessing
In every way and form,
We lived life to the fullest
Through the good times
And the storms.

Love is what the world's about,
It's love, and only love.
Just accept and love yourself,
Love's flowing from above.

Love is floating everywhere,
It's colour, wind and Light.
Embrace yourself and all you are
Love makes our world feel right.

Affirmation:

It's okay to take grieving time.

Remember I'm Still with You

When I leave this cosmos,
Please don't be forlorn.
Know that I'm still with you
Just in another form.

My body was my temple,
Just for a short time.
My spirit lived within it
Now to Heaven I climb.

From celestial realms I am with you,
Though to most, I am unseen.
Remember I'm still with you,
Just returned to where I've been.

You will join me one day,
Until then, you have my love.
Embrace your time upon this earth
I am here and there, above.

Affirmation:

I accept the things I cannot change.

Reunited

As I walk along the seashore,
I see the seagulls spring,
Soar up from the ocean
What wild songs they sing.

Perhaps they're singing to my friend
Whose life has passed away,
He would not wish for heavy hearts
Or thoughts in disarray.

My aim is to remind me
This person is at peace,
Has returned to where he started,
But his journey has not ceased.

His spirit is still with me,
His smile is bright and strong.
He's free from pain and suffering,
Back, where he belongs.

Reunited with his loved ones,
He will take some time to rest
I know that we will meet again,
Feel happy, not depressed.

Affirmation:

I am thankful for the time we shared.

Not the End

Death is really not the end,
It's just a new beginning.
The beginning of a new time
Before our next adventure.

Death is simply when we move
From one room to the other.
Our body completes this human life,
Our soul moves up to Heaven.

I'm reminded of the contract
That we view before our birth.
Aspire to a happy place,
Not a place of pain and hurt.

Affirmation:

I give thanks for living and loving.

Light Shines on Forever

I understand our essence lives
Completely and forever.
Sadness fades, Light pervades
No fear whatsoever.

Souls don't want us to be sad
When they leave a body,
Our spirit lives eternally,
Light shines on forever.

I don't believe that death's the end,
It's just a new beginning
Our lives are a learning time,
Now time for thanks giving.

Affirmation:

I embrace the love and Light which surrounds me.

My Friend

Please sit with me a moment,
As we reflect upon your life.
No words are really needed
It's all about your Light.

Your Light, it was contagious.
We all loved you to be near.
Your music and your caring words,
Were sacred to our ears.

Your students, friends and family,
Embraced your glowing face.
Wherever you walked upon this earth,
You displayed such loving grace.

Your inner glow was radiant,
Your heart and soul ... delight!
All seemed to be in perfect flow.
Everything felt right.

We know that you're at peace now,
At peace with Pop and Gran.
We'll miss your caring presence,
As God takes you by the hand.

We look forward to uniting,
When the time is right.
Play your drums, spread your wings
Soar, as your soul takes flight.

Affirmation:

My holiday doesn't have to be spent in the same as way others. are.

Happy Christmas

Christmas is a happy time.
Well, is that really so?
Depends on how I look at it,
The season leaves me feeling low.

I remember all the happy times,
Little children, gifts and fun.
Now, when Christmas is drawing near
I feel I want to run.

Run away from what? I ask.
A question deep to ponder.
What part of Christmas gets to me?
And which part should I honour?

The birth of Jesus is a fact.
That's what Christmas is.
Bring my thoughts back to new birth,
It's now time to forgive.

It isn't easy to forgive when
Hurt has taken place.
I will focus on the Christmas birth,
Replace conflict in mind with faith.

Affirmation:

I choose to spend Christmas however I desire.

Christmas Time

I loved Christmas morning
When I had two little kids,
They'd wake up at the crack of dawn
To open up their things.

The pillow-slips were bulging,
There were shrieks of Oh and Ah,
As they opened up their presents
You could hear them from afar.

Christmas Day is different now
It's quieter, more subdued.
It's a time for quiet reflection
Just me and cat Nero to include.

I reflect upon the pockets
As I think back on my life
Happy times, sometimes sad
It's my thoughts that make me wise.

Affirmation:

*I am grateful for new birth. I manifest
new positive opportunities.*

New Birth

An infant in a stable
A brilliant shining star,
Shepherds, seers and wise men
Coming from afar.

Jesus' birth is Light-filled
That's what people need.
Not to speculate and exploit
Christmas story plants a seed.

To focus on a new birth,
And everything that's good,
That's what Christmas is to me,
Doesn't have to be understood.

Author's Notes

Life is a series of peaks and troughs. We meet people along the way who are instrumental in our growth. We make decisions which are right for us at the time. As a retired civil celebrant, I thought it wise when my clients didn't wish to include until death us do part in their marriage vows. We grow together, we learn and we change.

My formal education was limited. I didn't allow this to hinder my achievements.

I explored several areas of sales and marketing before updating my qualifications at TAFE when I was in my fifties. I operated my own event management business based in Melbourne, taught advertising and marketing subjects at a tertiary level, became an authorized civil celebrant and while in my sixties delivered Job Search Training within the JobNetwork.

In the late 1980s I went through a stressful time in my life. A friend suggested I explore meditation. I took to it like a duck to water. The rewards were magical. I didn't realise how unrelaxed I was. We all meditate in our own way. It's just a matter of learning a few simple and natural techniques to help us discover our own way.

I began teaching Learn to Relax techniques at The Council of Adult Education (CAE) in the 1990s. I did this until I moved to the Bellarine Peninsula in 2011. Watching participants in my meditation groups grow and become more confident was gratifying.

My two children, grandchildren, friends, clients and students have all fuelled my inspiration for writing this book, which has evolved over a period of just a few months. It wasn't planned. It just happened. I had no inclination to write poetry until the words just came bubbling out from somewhere, *Where Love Is*. I'm eighty-one!

Jennifer

About the Author

The Presbyterian church in Portland was a significant part of my early years. In later years I studied meditation under the guidance of Sri Chinmoy. The teachings of the Buddha have also interested me. We are all guided to whatever philosophy or belief is right for us. Ultimately, the real teacher is the Good within all of us. After teaching meditation in Melbourne at Council of Adult Education (CAE) for many years, I now enjoy facilitating meditation groups as a community service on the Bellarine Peninsula.

Acknowledgements

Cindy Turnbow, Essence Of The Soul Healing, for her expansive insights.

Carolyn Morwood, for her encouragement and tireless editing.